70032
Leach Library

DISCARD

W9-BRM-647

DISCARD

Leach Library
276 Mammoth Road
Londonderry, NH 03053

Adult Services 432-1132
Children's Services 432-1127

A ROOKIE READER®

A WHISPER IS QUIET

By Carolyn Lunn

Illustrations by Clovis Martin

Prepared under the direction of Robert Hillerich, Ph.D.

 CHILDRENS PRESS®

CHICAGO

JE
LUN

99 June 23
Grolier CP
1700 (1275)

LIBRARY OF CONGRESS
Library of Congress Cataloging-in-Publication Data

Lunn, Carolyn.
    A whisper is quiet / by Carolyn Lunn.

        p. cm. — (A Rookie Reader)
    Summary: Presents pairs of things with contrasting
qualities, such as the hot sun and cold ice cream, or a
quiet whisper and a loud band.
    ISBN 0-516-02087-0
    1. English language—Synonyms and antonyms—
Juvenile literature. [1. English language—Synonyms
and antonyms.] I. Title. II. Series.
PE1591.L86   1988
428.1—dc19   88-11968
                                                                CIP
                                                                AC

Childrens Press®, Chicago
Copyright © 1988 by Regensteiner Publishing Enterprises, Inc.
All rights reserved. Published simultaneously in Canada.
Printed in the United States of America.
    11 12 13 14 15 16 17 18 19 R 02 01 00 99 98

A whisper is quiet.

A band is loud.

Two is a couple.

And a lot is a crowd.

An airplane is fast.

Rowboats are slow.

Red means stop.

Green means go!

Elephants are big.

A puppy is small.

Some clowns are short
and some are tall.

The sun is hot.

Ice cream is cold.

28

Who likes a parade?

The young and the old!

WORD LIST

a	crowd	loud	small
airplane	elephants	means	some
an	fast	old	stop
and	go	parade	sun
are	green	puppy	tall
band	hot	quiet	the
big	ice cream	red	two
clowns	is	rowboats	whisper
cold	likes	short	who
couple	lot	slow	young

About the Author

Carolyn Lunn is an American, now living in England with her British husband and two-year-old son. As well as writing stories, she enjoys running, cooking, and gardening. She also has written another Rookie Reader, *Purple Is Part of a Rainbow*.

About the Artist

Clovis Martin has enjoyed a varied career as a managing art director, art teacher, and freelance designer and illustrator serving major clients and national publications. He enjoys most illustrating for children and has produced a variety of educational materials and books. A graduate of the Cleveland Institute of Art, he resides with his wife and two children in Cleveland Heights, Ohio.